··A·Kitten·A·week··

··A·Kitten·A·Week··

*Fifty-Two Quips and Quotations about
Young Felines from the
English Literary Tradition*

Compiled by Sted Mays
Designed by Charles Björklund

BALLANTINE
BOOKS

NEW YORK

Copyright © 1994 by Sted Mays

Illustrations copyright © 1994 by Charles Björklund

All rights reserved under International and Pan-American Copyright Conventions. Published in the United States by Ballantine Books, a division of Random House, Inc., New York, and simultaneously in Canada by Random House of Canada Limited, Toronto.

Library of Congress Catalog Card Number:93-90549

ISBN:0-345-38704-X

Cover art, original illustrations, and design copyright ©1994 by Charles Björklund

Manufactured in the United States of America

First Edition: April 1994

10 9 8 7 6 5 4 3 2 1

For our Mothers,
Barbara and Beeps

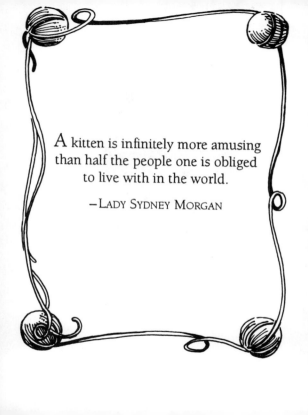

A kitten is infinitely more amusing
than half the people one is obliged
to live with in the world.

—LADY SYDNEY MORGAN

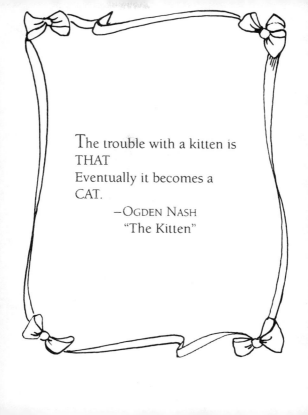

The trouble with a kitten is
THAT
Eventually it becomes a
CAT.

—OGDEN NASH
"The Kitten"

A kitten is so flexible that she is almost double; the hind parts are equivalent to another kitten with which the forepart plays. She does not discover that her tail belongs to her until you tread upon it.

–HENRY DAVID THOREAU
Journal Entry

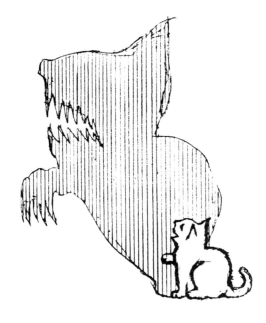

The kitten, indeed, is an irresistible bundle of animate fur, all nerves and tenderness, all play-actor, dashing madly against nothing,...chasing his tail, making a vain attempt to capture and worry his own shadow.

—CARL VAN VECHTEN
The Tiger in the House

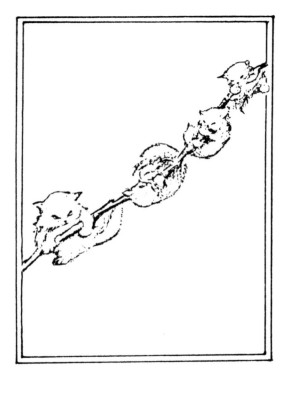

I sometimes think the
            Pussy-Willows grey
Are Angel Kittens who
            have lost their way,
And every Bulrush on
            the river bank
A Cat-Tail from some
            lovely Cat astray.

—OLIVER HERFORD
The Rubaiyat of a Persian Kitten

A little Girl asked some kittens
        to tea,
To meet some Dolls from France;
And the Mother came, too, to enjoy
        a view
And afterwards play for the dance.
But the Kittens were rude & grabbed
        their food
And treated the Dolls with jeers;
Which caused the Mother an aching heart
And seven or eight large tears.

                    —J. G. FRANCIS
                    "The Tea-Party"

what in hell
have I done to deserve...

...all these kittens

–DON MARQUIS
archy and mehitabel

kittens cuddle coyishly clinging
cringing coquettishly consuming
catnippish confraternal cordials
creaking clawing cutting crying coalescing:
confrontational crises that never happen.

–PEARL JARED CLARK
"basketed litter of kittens"

Ez soshubble ez a baskit
er kittens.

–JOEL CHANDLER HARRIS
Uncle Remus and His Friends

A kitten is a thing apart; and many people who lack the discriminating enthusiasm for cats, who regard these beautiful beasts with aversion and mistrust, are won over easily, and cajoled out of their prejudices by the deceitful wiles of kittenhood.

—AGNES REPPLIER
"A Kitten"

A young cat or kitten is graceful; her
chief occupation is chasing her tail,
but her tail will not stay chased.
Very little children adore
very little cats.

—EDGAR ALLAN POE
"Desultory Notes on Cats"

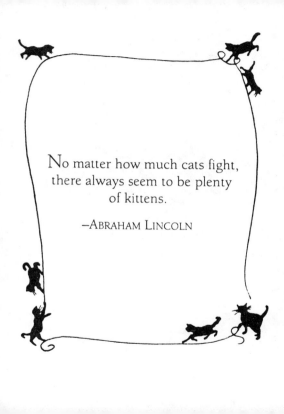

No matter how much cats fight,
there always seem to be plenty
of kittens.

—ABRAHAM LINCOLN

The kitten sleeps upon the hearth,
The crickets long have ceased their mirth;

There's nothing stirring in the house
Save one *wee*, hungry, nibbling mouse...

—DOROTHY WORDSWORTH
"The Cottager to Her Infant"

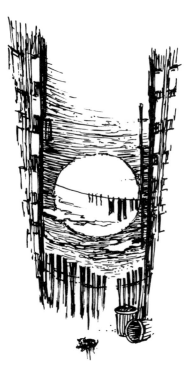

...we have seen
The moon in lonely alleys make
A grail of laughter of an empty
    ash can,
And through all sound of gaiety
    and quest
Have heard a kitten in the
    wilderness.

—HART CRANE
"Chaplinesque"

It's a wild's kitten, my dear,
who can tell a wilkling from
a warthog.

—JAMES JOYCE
Finnegans Wake

A black-nosed
kitten
will slumber
all the day;

A white-nosed
kitten
is ever glad
to play;

A yellow-nosed | And a gray-nosed
kitten | kitten
will answer to | I wouldn't have
your call; | at all.

—ANONYMOUS
"To One Choosing a Kitten"

Kitten, kitten, two months old,
Woolly snowball lying snug,
Curl'd up in the warmest fold
Of the warm hearth-rug,
Turn your drowsy head this way.
What is life? O kitten, say!

—THOMAS WESTWOOD
"Kitten Gossip"

The brisk mouse may feast herself
     with crumbs,
Till that the green-ey'd
     kitling comes.

–ROBERT HERRICK
"A Country Life: To His Brother"

The burning yellow eyes of inky-black kittens
Glow like Halloween lanterns
After midnight.

Their phosphorescent irises glisten and gleam,
Sending beams that illumi-
Nate Nocturnal
Dreams

—STUART MASON
"Nocturne"

Purrrrrrrrrrrrrrrr

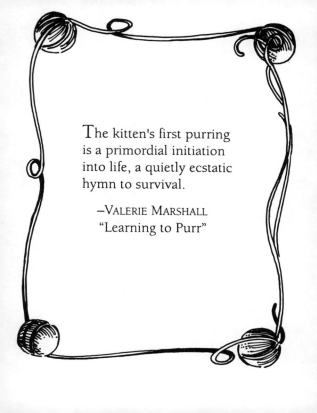

The kitten's first purring
is a primordial initiation
into life, a quietly ecstatic
hymn to survival.

–VALERIE MARSHALL
"Learning to Purr"

The joy felt when watching
the face of a young kitten is the
profound joy of bringing back
to the surface, for a moment at
least, the inner-child that we
all harbor secretly inside.

—TWELVE-STEP PROGRAM MEMBER

The Kitten, how she starts,
Crouches, stretches, paws, and darts!...
Were her antics played in the eye
Of a thousand standers-by,
Clapping hands with shout and stare,
What would little Tabby care
For the plaudits of the crowd?
Over happy to be proud,
Over wealthy in the treasure
Of her own exceeding pleasure!

—WILLIAM WORDSWORTH
"The Kitten and Falling Leaves"

Old Pussy, grave Pussy,
    Sat by the fire;
Little Kitty, pretty Kitty,
    Came and sat by her.

Old Pussy, grave Pussy,
    Put out her paw;
Little Kitty, frisky Kitty,
    Gave it a claw.

Old Pussy, grave Pussy,
    Shook her wise head;
Little Kitty, naughty Kitty,
    Wouldn't mind a word she said.

—TRADITIONAL NURSERY
    RHYME

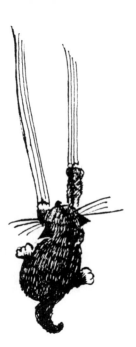

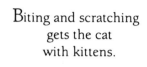

Biting and scratching
gets the cat
with kittens.

—PROVERB

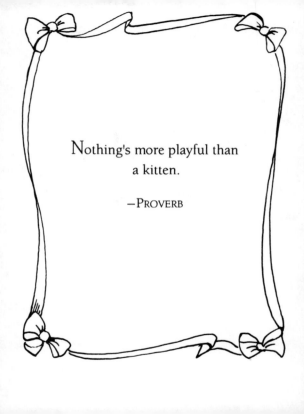

Nothing's more playful than
a kitten.

—Proverb

Who will play with Jane?
See the cat. It goes meow-meow.
Come and play. Come play with Jane.
The kitten will not play...see the cat it
goes meow-meow come and play
come play with jane the kitten will
not play...

motherfatherdickandjaneliveinthe
greenandwhitehousetheyarevery
happyseejaneshehasareddressshe
wantstoplaywhowillplaywithjanesee
thecatitgoesmeowmeowcomeandplay
comeplaywithjanethekittenwill
notplay...

    —TONI MORRISON
    The Bluest Eye

"Kit's Cradle" (A Kitten Speaks)

They've taken the cosy bed away
That I made myself with the
    Shetland shawl,
And set me a hamper of scratchy
    hay,
By that great black stove in the
    entrance-hall.

I won't sleep there; I'm resolved
    on that!
They may think I will, but they
    little know
There's a soft persistence about
    a cat
That even a little kitten can show.

–JULIANA A. EWING

Confront a child, a puppy, and a kitten with a sudden danger; the child will turn instinctively for assistance, the puppy will grovel in abject submission, the kitten will brace its tiny body for a frantic resistance.

–H. H. MUNRO ("Saki")
The Achievement of the Cat

Trembling, I've seen thee dare the
kitten's paw...

—Alexander Pope
"The Lamentation of Glumdalclitch"

What, though no mice are caught by a
     young kitten,
May it not leap and play as grown cats do,
Till its claws come?

—PERCY BYSSHE SHELLEY
"The Witch of Atlas"

Dear kitten, do lie still, I say,

For much I want you to be quiet,

Instead of scampering away,

And always making such a riot!

—ANN TAYLOR
"The Frolicsome Kitten"

There is one order of beauty which seems made to turn the heads not only of men, but of all intelligent mammals, even of women. It is a beauty like that of kittens...a beauty with which you can never be angry, but

that you feel ready to crush for
inability to comprehend the
state of mind into which it
throws you.

—GEORGE ELIOT
(MARY ANN EVANS)
Adam Bede

Thou art beautiful as ever cat
That wanton'd in the joy of
kittenhood.

—ROBERT SOUTHEY
Nondescripts

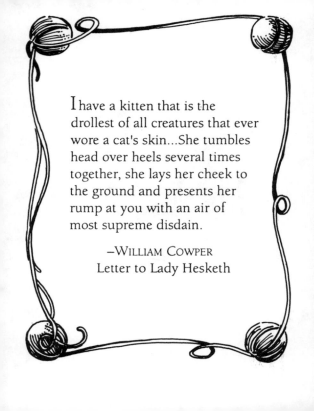

I have a kitten that is the
drollest of all creatures that ever
wore a cat's skin...She tumbles
head over heels several times
together, she lays her cheek to
the ground and presents her
rump at you with an air of
most supreme disdain.

–WILLIAM COWPER
Letter to Lady Hesketh

Do you see that kitten chasing
so prettily her own tail? If you
could look with her eyes, you
might see her surrounded with
hundreds of figures performing
complex dramas, with tragic
and comic issues, long
conversations, many characters,
many ups and downs of fate.

—RALPH WALDO EMERSON
Experience

Be not amazed
    to see God's eye
        in the eye of
            the kitten.

—ANONYMOUS

Hey, my kitten, my kitten,
    And hey my kitten, my deary!
Such a sweet pet as this
    There is not far nor neary.
Here we go up, up, up,
    Here we go down, down, downy;
Here we go backwards and forwards,
    And here we go round, round, roundy.

—AUTHOR UNKNOWN

The Kitten too was comical,
She play'd so oddly with her tail.

—WILLIAM WHITEHEAD
Variety

♫ SONG OF A KITTEN ON A SWING

I'm just a kitten on a swing,
Can't understand the words I sing,
Mommy-cat gave me no feather to wing—
A kitten on a swing!

I watch the birdies in the air,
Flying about without a care,
What would I give for that chance
    O so rare—
A kitten on a swing!

When I feel the air rushing round,
And I'm off the ground,
Then I sing in a voice that soars through
    the spheres.

But I'm just a kitten on a swing,
Can't understand the words I sing,
Mommy-cat gave me no feather to wing—
A kitten on a swing!

—CHILDREN'S SONG

"The Looking-Glass Pussy
(The Kitten Speaks)"

Back behind the mirror is another
    pussy-cat
With bows and whiskers just like mine,
    and just as gray and fat.

She peeps around and looks at me when
    I peep in at her,
And looks as pleased as possible
    each time she hears me purr.

She pats her paws against the glass
    when I pat mine there too;
But she won't come and play with me,
    no matter how I mew!

—MARGARET WIDDEMER

When I was a very young kitten I had the misfortune to lose my mother and find myself alone in the world at the age of six weeks. However, I was not unduly disturbed by this, since I was intelligent, not ill-favored, resourceful and full of confidence in myself.

—PAUL GALLICO
The Silent Miaow

I love little kitty,
    Her coat is so warm,
And if I don't hurt her
    She'll do me no harm.
So I'll not pull her tail,
    Nor drive her away,
But kitten and I
    Very gently will play.

—TRADITIONAL NURSERY RHYME

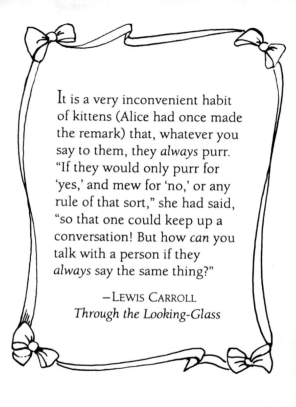

It is a very inconvenient habit of kittens (Alice had once made the remark) that, whatever you say to them, they *always* purr. "If they would only purr for 'yes,' and mew for 'no,' or any rule of that sort," she had said, "so that one could keep up a conversation! But how *can* you talk with a person if they *always* say the same thing?"

—LEWIS CARROLL
Through the Looking-Glass

Come, pussy, will you learn to read,
　　I've got a pretty book?
Nay, turn this way, you must indeed —
　　Fie, there's sulky look.

Here is a pretty picture, see,
　　An apple, and great A:
How stupid you will ever be,
　　If you do nought but play.

—JANE TAYLOR
"The Dunce of a Kitten"

Wanton kittens may

make sober old cats.

—PROVERB

I had a kitten—I was rich
In pets—but all too soon my kitten
Became a full-sized cat, by which
I've more than once been scratched and bitten.

—CHARLES S. CALVERLY
"Disaster"

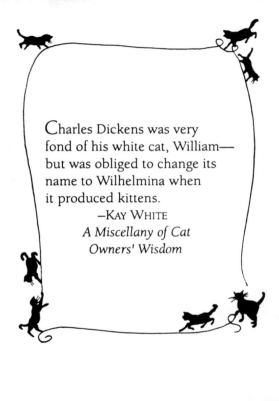

Charles Dickens was very fond of his white cat, William— but was obliged to change its name to Wilhelmina when it produced kittens.

–KAY WHITE
A Miscellany of Cat Owners' Wisdom

He hastily cut the string and removed the lid of the box, and inside, reposing on a nest of hay, lay a very young and mewey kitten. A kitten who most evidently was homesick and aggrieved at being reft from the maternal bosom. A sprawly, squirmy, noisy kitten...

—Mr. Neatby receives an unexpected package in L. ALLEN HARKER'S "The Vagaries of Tod and Peter"

For we can still love the world, who find
A famished kitten on the step, and know
Recesses for it from the fury of the street...

—HART CRANE
"Chaplinesque"

Were I endowed with the power
of suspending the effect of time upon
the things around me, methinks there
are some of my flowers which should
neither fall nor fade: decidedly my
kitten should never attain to cathood.

—ROBERT SOUTHEY
The Doctor

The three merriest things
in the world are a cat's kitten, a
goat's kid, and a young widow.

—IRISH PROVERB

I had rather
be a Kitten
and cry mew...

—WILLIAM SHAKESPEARE
Henry IV, Part One

THE 	END

Grateful acknowledgment is made to the following for permission to reprint material:

Pearl Jared Clark. "basketed litter of kittens," copyright ©1994 by Pearl Jared Clark.

Hart Crane. The lines from "Chaplinesque" are reprinted from *The Complete Poems and Selected Letters and Prose of Hart Crane,* edited by Brom Weber, by permission of Liveright Publishing Corporation. Copyright 1933, ©1958, 1966 by Liveright Publishing Corporation.

Don Marquis. "mehitabel and her kittens," from *archy and mehitabel,* copyright © 1927 by Doubleday, a division of Bantam Doubleday Dell Publishing Group, Inc.

Stuart Mason. "Nocturne," from *The Lyrical Cat: A Book of Original Feline Verse* (work in progress), copyright ©1994 by Stuart Mason.

Barbara Noel McFerrin. "Song of a Kitten on a Swing," words and music copyright©1994 by Barbara Noel McFerrin.

Ogden Nash. "The Kitten," from *Verses from 1929 On,* copyright 1940 by Ogden Nash. By permission of Little, Brown and Company. In the world excluding North America, "The Kitten" is reprinted by permission of Curtis Brown, Ltd. from *Many Long Years Ago.* Copyright ©1945 by Ogden Nash.

Margaret Widdemer. "The Looking-Glass Pussy" from *Little Girl and Boy Land* by Margaret Widdemer, copyright 1924 by Harcourt Brace & Company and renewed 1952 by Margaret Widdemer Schauffler, reprinted by permission of the publisher.